Mothballs

Mothballs
Quantum Poems

Seb Doubinsky

Leaky Boot Press

Mothballs: Quantum Poems
by Seb Doubinsky

First published in 2013 by
Leaky Boot Press
http://www.leakyboot.com

Copyright © 2013 Seb Doubinsky
All rights reserved

No part of this book may be reproduced or transmitted in any form or by any means, electronic, mechanical, photocopying, recording, or otherwise, without prior written permission of the author.

ISBN: 978-1-909849-00-6

Contents

Acknowledgements	7
Poem With a View	12
What Body Is	13
A Postcard to Cynthia	15
The Way	18
Transition	20
Either Or	21
A House Deconstructed	22
The Little Things That Break	23
Sunset Sunup	24
Nausicaa	28
Familiar	30
Claro Que Si	31
Dead Beat	34
Apex	35
Dog	37
Iolanthe	38
Iskander	39
From Bagdad to Kabul	40
Landscape Impro	42
Open Hands	43
Pink Bicycle	50
Lawnmower Satori	51
I Want to Sing	62
Seasons	64
Soviet Supreme	65
Broken Heart—Technical Failure	66
Zen and the Art of Poetry	71

Acknowledgements

Some of these poems have previously appeared in the following online reviews and magazines: Earthen Lamp Journal, Coldnoon, DIOGEN, and the Four Quarters Magazine.

poetry
limits
silence

head full of noise
heart full of noise
empty hands

my lungs are old
but my breath
is even older

Poem With a View

my eyes are open
the sun is shining
yet I see nothing
because my eyes
haven't been told
what they should see
-my soul laughs
at my stupid eyes
before picking up its white cane
and grabbing me by the arm
for our daily walk

What Body Is

What body is

inside bones
outside crust

the noise of machine

and fluids

*

What body is

a something that doesn't want
to be anything yet is

a concept embodied

a flash of lightning

*

What body is

mine and yours and mine
again

messages and fingers

a thought misspelled

*

What body is

a perfumed furnace
a diamond factory

a wanting tongue

a pause

*

What body is

an image set in negative inside the brain
an everlasting sensation of something once held

a darkness desired

a mountain to climb and fall from

*

What body is

a soft prison decorated with obscene graffiti
a porn theater that smells of you and you only

a hot summer fair

a piercing flute melody

*

What body is

I don't know and have never known
closed eyelids do not offer comfort
but my mouth on your hair does

my mouth on your hair does

A Postcard to Cynthia

    paper mermaid
    faded sea
    blueing ink

time has no direction
and we are becoming as young
as we are becoming old
our soul pulled fourways
by the music that still haunts us

the church bells ring
the summer sky
mirrors
their emptiness

The Way

Every stone on
the path is rich
with the promise
of violence

sun heat
slow thoughts
delayed shadows

Transition

The sound of a bell
in the busy afternoon

A bird not seen
but only guessed

A gesture planned
but not achieved

The door is half-open

I stand up and walk towards
the morning light

I close the door
behind me

and hesitate

Either Or

Two stones shine
under the surface of the stream

Where is my
reflection?

A House Deconstructed

The roof
the wal
ls
the base
ment
a famil
y
no
car
no t
v
n
o
thi
ng

The Little Things That Break

When we were children
do you remember
stepping on a plastic princess ring,
on a little red car or just any tiny toy
that broke with a snap?
Do you remember the pain that shot
through your foot up to your brain,
destroying every single nerve and cell,
bringing water to your eyes
and twist your lips into an agonizing cry?
Later, we would break bigger things,
like stereos and tvs and cars
and friendships and marriages
and our illusions and ourselves
- But still, we will never, ever, forget
The little things that break

Sunset Sunup

Neons never set
but they die
and become
colored glass
- empty
colored
glass
reflecting
nothing
underneath
the dust

slow morning
half-hearted sky
glowing heartbeat

warm evening
whispers drift
stars tremble

cool breeze
sea rustles
soul tightens

Nausicaa

White softness of the arms
under the drowned man's salty shoulders
Mythical grains of sand washed by the waves
silent witnesses forever forgotten
But forever forgotten
also
the woman the girl
who brought out
from the surf
the story
to be told

language has no direction
clouds fly backwards
as I write
swallowed whole
by the blue sky
swallowed whole
all of us
by the limited infinites
we call words

Familiar

The possibility
of a cat in the shadow
and the whisper of the rain
on the window pane
– At home
yet not completely
at home

Claro Que Si

To Claro

To translate
is to make
other noises
sound like
other noises

poetry is like
lead, radioactivity,
quicksilver
in small doses
in our bones
– invisible, yet there
heavy, lethal, beautiful

cracked back
beautiful sunrise
beauty in disharmony

Dead Beat

Leave the dust
on the road,
friend
Leave it
where
it belongs

Apex

The city shines
like a broken bottle
evoking blood
and the faint smell
of puke

Death is not
an absence

Death is just
another form
of presence

just like
a crack
in the glass

or
a pair
of new
shoes

Dog

I don't wa
nt
a leash I
want a bon
e

Iolanthe

To Lawrence Durrell

Her heart is shaped
as a hook

His mouth half-open

Willing

Iskander

The future
offers nothing
Only the past
holds promises

From Bagdad to Kabul

Blood has a different hue
under some suns
and the words we use
to name things
suddenly
name other things

Hostile territory
becomes the metaphor
of a dead soldier
and a laughing crowd

And yes, we will be
remembered
unfortunately
we will be
remembered

But although
our weapons
shine like bronze
we will
not
become myth

I trip
a pile of books fall
-Babel

Landscape Impro

To Yannis Livadas

This city is flat
C-flat

Open Hands

    one hand   the other hand
the other hand   one hand

closed mouth
open mind
closed eyes
open mouth
- poetry switch

consciousness filters
through my eyes
like slow electricity
- poetry sparkles inwards

rain paints
the world grey
-old chinese ink

after the rain
the clouds
flap like torn sheets
-cleanliness of the soul

the sun tries to shine
through the white fogged-up windows
sometimes light is like thoughts

No words for me today
the earth is as flat
as the sky
and the birds
have left their songs
hanging in the trees

Pink Bicycle

To WCW

the sun turns
blinding
the circling sparrows

the wind
dries
the leaves still on the branch

a few clouds
drift by
like Tour de France champions

this bicycle
leaning
on the corner
of the large house
has no shadow

Lawnmower Satori

To Pierre Bourgeais

last time I mow the grass
before the winter

impossible
to think straight
with that metallic
racket

the smell
of chopped grass
fills
my nostrils

green tickle

the lawnmower's engine
sounds like a moped

Peugeot 103

teenage spree
in the empty streets
of Tours
at two o'clock
in the morning

unlikely transparencies
of a Sunday morning

things vibrate
at incredible speed
—a knife, an apple

my father died
thirteen years ago

I miss my father
like when I was
a child
waiting
for him
to come back
from a trip

but when I was a child
I was mostly waiting
for the presents
he would bring back

today
I would be contented
by his mere presence

when dawn rips
like a pair of old jeans
you realize that life
is beyond repair

our words fail
we are slowly
replaced by
electricity
and a nostalgia
of ourselves
we are
becoming
here and then
we are
becoming
remembered

low clouds
high trees
elliptic birds
my breath settles
and becomes machine

to return is not to come back
it is to be where you haven't been before
like the rain brought by the wind on the roof
or grass growing over forgotten steps

words travel faster than light
even if our hands and tongue
are heavier than air
and tied by shadows

two words
one poem
many possibilities

closing shop
-dying eyes
of the sun

I Want to Sing

To Matt Bialer

I want to sing a song anybody can sing and hum even those who do not know how to sing or hum

I want to sing about things and stuff you can find if you bend over the sidewalk

I want to sing about dog shits and broken pearl necklaces the smell of sex and the sweet ocean wind

I want to sing of crumpled cigarette packages and the death of heroes that I have chosen to be heroes

I want to sing of words heavy as two kilos of sugar and dark as dark coffee I want to sing about words that keep you awake at night

I want to sing about UFOs ghosts and werewolves about a child that cringes at night and talks to the stars

I want to sing in various languages some of them ancient some of them impossible some of them crazy babble some of them French

I want to sing about women with tight cunts large cunts or no cunts at all

I want to sing about men with tight cunts large cunts or no cunts at all

I want to sing

I want to sing the depth of my voice when it is at rest
I want to sing the pitch of my silent scream

I want to sing yes I want to sing a song with no music no words and no rhymes

A song with nothing but itself and me in the middle somewhere singing

Seasons

O castles

*

flat heavy sky
car exhausts
–summer

*

a cold breeze
remember to buy instant coffee
–fall

*

O castles

*

frozen windshield
the laughter of children
–winter

*

A season in hell
the smell of warmed up pages
–spring

*

O castles

Soviet Supreme

    all systems petrify
    poetry too
    do does
    a crack of the knuckles
    that's it

Broken Heart—Technical Failure

to write is silence
to speak is no silence
to think is silence outside
to no speak is silence outside
to no write is no silence
- to no exist is no write no speak is silence
to exist is noise write/no write speak/no speak
love/no love think/no think here/no here
where there no nowhere there
right there

hesitation is a moment
between kingdom and catastrophe
– all of our humanity
concentrated in
a stutter of the mind

morning poetry
everything crumbles
at my feet

paper bones
paper dust
white desert

a thought about death,
coffee, love and the passing of clouds

Zen and the Art of Poetry

     an arrow shot
     a target missed
     depth of the grass

words resist
until they give way
-free fall

snow roofs
blue wind
yellow hands
and a few black crows
to punctuate the morning hours

war on television
snow storm here
–the indifference of nature
and electricity

frozen water
-my poetry
reflects nothing

rumors of apocalypse
christmas carols blasting in the shops
– ah the huge boredom of the West

drunk poets
confusing words
new year

here we are
sitting around the table
drinking our instant death
and waiting for the weather
to tell us what to do
– the half-moon stands still
unaware of its heart-wrenching beauty

snow melts
cat sleeps
radio on
information overflow

poem finished
poet rewrites
poem finished

everything in its perfect place
words fall where they should
only the sky is oblique

objects
like poetry
move faster
than the eyes
can see

sun rises
sky bluens
day clicks

white sky
poet writes
white clouds

objects matter
but are
dead things

images matter
but are
dead things

life is
another word
for death

gravity pulls
our souls
into ourselves

poets!
never underestimate
the materiality of words
and the void of things
the soul hangs in between
-tongue hands breath

my bones are beats
my bits are gone
beats of bony bits
beasts of bones

one bird
two birds
one branch
one tree
no birds
one poem

pope gone
money gone
bus arriving

poetry
emits
silence

www.ingramcontent.com/pod-product-compliance
Lightning Source LLC
Chambersburg PA
CBHW030003050426
42451CB00006B/102